This Book Belongs To:

_____

The Rand McNally Book of
Favorite
Nursery Rhymes

RAND McNALLY & COMPANY · Chicago

Established 1856

CONTENTS

THREE LITTLE KITTENS

Three little kittens
lost their mittens,
And they began to cry,
"Oh, Mother dear,
We very much fear
That we have lost our
mittens."

"Lost your mittens!
You naughty kittens!
Then you shall have no pie!"

"Mee-ow, mee-ow, mee-ow."
"No, you shall have no pie."
"Mee-ow, mee-ow, mee-ow."

The three little kittens
found their mittens,
And they began to cry,

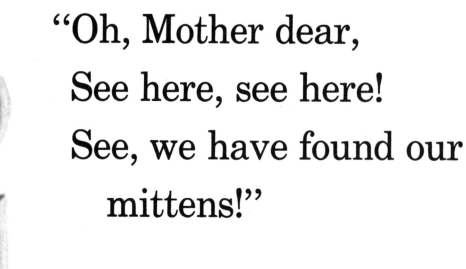

"Oh, Mother dear,
  See here, see here!
  See, we have found our
    mittens!"

"Put on your mittens,
  You silly kittens,
  And you may have some pie."

"Purr-r, purr-r, purr-r,
Oh, let us have the pie!
Purr-r, purr-r, purr-r."

The three little kittens
    put on their mittens,
And soon ate up the pie;

"Oh, Mother dear,
We greatly fear
That we have soiled our
    mittens!"

"Soiled your mittens!
You naughty kittens!"

Then they began to sigh,
"Mee-ow, mee-ow, mee-ow."
Then they began to sigh,
"Mee-ow, mee-ow, mee-ow."

The three little kittens
washed their mittens,
And hung them out to dry;

"Oh, Mother dear,
  Do you not hear
  That we have washed our
    mittens?"

"Washed your mittens!
   Oh, you're good kittens!
   But I smell a rat close by.
   Hush, hush! Mee-ow, mee-ow."

"We smell a rat close by,
   Mee-ow, mee-ow, mee-ow."

WYNKEN, BLYNKEN, AND NOD

Wynken, Blynken, and Nod one night
    Sailed off in a wooden shoe,
Sailed on a river of crystal light,
    Into a sea of dew.
"Where are you going,
      and what do you wish?"
    The old moon asked the three.
"We have come to fish for the herring fish
    That live in this beautiful sea—
Nets of silver and gold have we!"
    Said Wynken, Blynken, and Nod.

The old moon laughed and sang a song,
    As they rocked in the wooden shoe,
And the wind that sped them
      all night long
    Ruffled the waves of dew.
The little stars were the herring fish
    That lived in that beautiful sea.
"Now cast your nets wherever you wish,
    Never afeard are we!"
    So cried the stars to
      the fishermen three:
Wynken, Blynken, and Nod.

All night long their nets they threw
　　To the stars in
　　　　the twinkling foam,
Then down from the skies
　　　　came the wooden shoe,
　　Bringing the fishermen home.
'T was all so pretty a sail it seemed
　　As if it could not be,
And some folks thought 't was
　　　　a dream they'd dreamed
　　Of sailing that beautiful sea,
But I shall name you
　　　　the fishermen three:
Wynken, Blynken, and Nod.

Wynken and Blynken are two little eyes,
And Nod is a little head,
And the wooden shoe that sailed the skies
Is a wee one's trundle bed.
So shut your eyes while Mother sings
Of wonderful sights that be,
And you shall see the beautiful things
As you rock in the misty sea,
Where the old shoe rocked
the fishermen three:
Wynken, Blynken, and Nod.

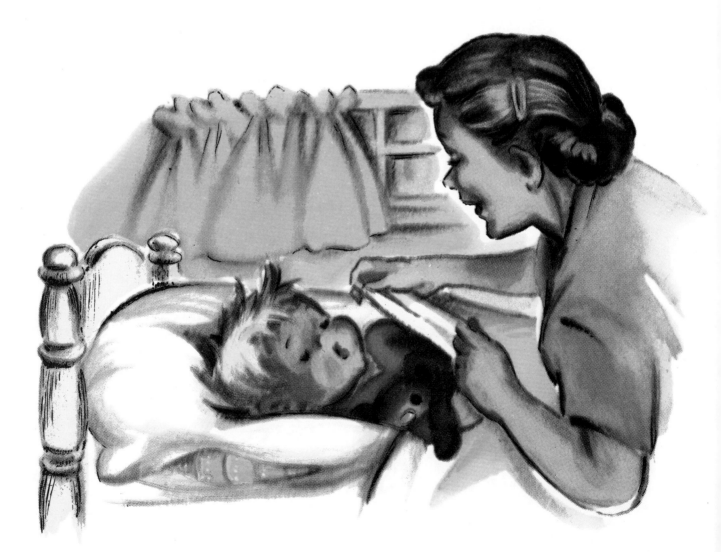

THE DRUM

I'm a beautiful, red, red drum,
    And I train with the soldier boys,
As up the street we come,
    Wonderful is our noise!
There's Tom, and Jim, and Phil,
    And Dick, and Nat, and Fred,

While Widow Cutler's Bill
And I march on ahead,
With a *r-r-rat-tat-tat*
And a *tum-titty-um-tum-tum*—
Oh, there's bushels of fun in that
For boys with a little red drum!

The Injuns came last night,
   While the soldiers were abed,
And they gobbled a Chinese kite
   And off to the woods they fled!
The woods are the cherry trees
   Down in the orchard lot,
And the soldiers are marching to seize
   The booty the Injuns got.
With *tum-titty-um-tum-tum*,
   And *r-r-rat-tat-tat*,
When soldiers marching come,
   Injuns had better scat!

THE SUGARPLUM TREE

Have you ever heard
      of the Sugarplum Tree?
'T is a marvel of great renown!
It blooms on the shore of the Lollipop Sea
      In the garden of Shut-Eye Town,
The fruit that it bears
      is so wondrously sweet
(As those who have tasted it say),
That good little children have only to eat
      Of that fruit to be happy next day.

There are marshmallows, gumdrops,
      and peppermint canes,
      With stripings of scarlet or gold,
And you carry away
      of the treasure that rains
As much as your apron can hold!

So come, little child, cuddle closer to me
In your dainty
   white nightcap and gown,
And I'll rock you away to that
   Sugarplum Tree
   In the garden of Shut-Eye Town.

THE DUEL

The gingham dog and the calico cat
Side by side on the table sat,
'T was half-past twelve and (what do you
think!)
Nor one nor t'other had slept a wink!
     The old Dutch clock
          and the Chinese plate
     Appeared to know as sure as fate
There was going to be a terrible spat.
     (*I wasn't there; I simply state*
     What was told to me
          by the Chinese plate!)

The gingham dog went, "Bow-wow-wow!"
And the calico cat replied, "Mee-ow!"
The air was littered, an hour or so,
With bits of gingham and calico,
    While the old Dutch clock
        in the chimney place
    Up with its hands before its face,
For it always dreaded a family row!
    (*Now mind: I'm only telling you*
    What the old Dutch clock
        declares is true!)

The Chinese plate looked very blue,
And wailed, "Oh, dear! what shall we do!"
But the gingham dog and the calico cat
Wallowed this way and tumbled that,
    Employing every tooth and claw
    In the awfullest way you ever saw,
And, oh! how the gingham and calico flew!
    (Don't fancy I exaggerate,
    I got my news from the Chinese plate!)

Next morning, where the two had sat,
They found no trace of dog or cat,
And some folks think unto this day
That burglars stole that pair away!
    But the truth about the cat and pup
    Is this: they ate each other up!
Now what do you really think of that!
    (The old Dutch Clock it told me so,
    And that is how I came to know.)

THE CUNNIN' LITTLE THING

When baby wakes of mornings,
Then it's wake, ye people all!
For another day
Of song and play
Has come at our darling's call!
And till she gets her dinner,
She makes the welkin ring,
And she *won't* keep still
till she's had her fill—
The cunnin' little thing!

FAIRY AND CHILD

Oh, listen, little Dear-My-Soul,
    To the fairy voices calling,
For the moon is high in the misty sky
    And the honey dew is falling;
To the midnight feast in the clover bloom
    The bluebells are a-ringing,
And it's "Come away to the Land of Fay"
    That the katydid is singing.

Oh, slumber, little Dear-My-Soul,
    And hand in hand we'll wander,
Hand in hand to the beautiful land
    Of Balow, away off yonder;
And you shall dance in the velvet sky,
    And the silvery stars shall twinkle
And dream sweet dreams
        as over their beams
    Your footfalls softly tinkle.

THE SHUT-EYE TRAIN

Come, my little one, with me!
There are wondrous sights to see
   As the evening shadows fall—
  In your pretty cap and gown,
     Don't detain
     The Shut-Eye train,
  "*Ting-a-ling!*" the bell it goeth,
  "*Toot-toot!*" the whistle bloweth,
And we hear the warning call,
"All aboard for Shut-Eye Town!"

Shut-Eye Town is passing fair,
Golden dreams await us there,
We shall dream
    those dreams, my dear,
Till the Mother Moon goes down—

See unfold
Delights untold!
And in those mysterious places
We shall see beloved faces
And beloved voices hear
In the grace of Shut-Eye Town.

THE CAT AND THE FIDDLE

Hey, diddle, diddle!
The cat and the fiddle,
The cow jumped over the moon;
The little dog laughed
To see such sport,
And the dish ran away with the spoon.

ONE, TWO, THREE

One, two, three, four, five,
Once I caught a fish alive.
Six, seven, eight, nine, ten,
But I let it go again.
Why did you let it go?
Because it bit my finger so.
Which finger did it bite?
The little one upon the righ

TWEEDLE-DUM AND
TWEEDLE-DEE

Tweedle-dum and Tweedle-dee
    Resolved to have a battle,
For Tweedle-dum said Tweedle-dee
    Had spoiled his nice new rattle.

Just then flew by a monstrous crow,
    As big as a tar barrel,
Which frightened both the heroes so,
    They quite forgot their quarrel.

JUST LIKE ME

"I went up one pair of stairs."
    "Just like me."

"I went up two pairs of stairs."
    "Just like me."

"I went into a room."
    "Just like me."

"I looked out of a window."
    "Just like me."

"And there I saw a monkey."
    "Just like me."

52

RIDE AWAY, RIDE AWAY

Ride away, ride away,
 Johnny shall ride,
And he shall have pussy-cat
 Tied to one side;
And he shall have little dog
 Tied to the other,
And Johnny shall ride
 To see his grandmother.

IF WISHES
WERE HORSES

If wishes were horses,
    beggars would ride.
If turnips were watches, I would
    wear one by my side.
And if "ifs" and "ands"
Were pots and pans,
There'd be no work for tinkers!

56

THE MAN OF BOMBAY

There was a fat man of Bombay,
Who was smoking one sunshiny day;
When a bird called a snipe
Flew away with his pipe,
Which vexed the fat man of Bombay.

BANBURY CROSS

Ride a cock-horse to Banbury Cross,
To see an old lady upon a white horse.
Rings on her fingers, and bells on her toes,
She shall have music wherever she goes.

PUSSY-CAT
AND THE DUMPLINGS

Pussy-cat ate the dumplings, the dumplings,
Pussy-cat ate the dumplings.
Mamma stood by, and cried, "Oh, fie!
Why did you eat the dumplings?"

DUCKS AND DRAKES

A duck and a drake,
And a halfpenny cake,
With a penny to pay the old baker.
A hop and a scotch
Is another notch,
Slitherum, slatherum, take her.

LOCK AND KEY

"I am a gold lock."
"I am a gold key."
"I am a silver lock."
"I am a silver key."
"I am a brass lock."
"I am a brass key."
"I am a lead lock."
"I am a lead key."
"I am a don lock."
"I am a don key."

62

THE GIRL IN THE LANE

The girl in the lane, that couldn't
speak plain,
Cried, "Gobble, gobble, gobble."
The man on the hill that couldn't
stand still,
Went hobble, hobble, hobble.

PUSSY-CAT
AND QUEEN

"Pussy-cat, pussy-cat,
    Where have you been?"
"I've been to London
    To look at the Queen."

"Pussy-cat, pussy-cat,
    What did you there?"
"I frightened a little mouse
    Under the chair."

COCK-A-DOODLE-DO!

Cock-a-doodle-do!
My dame has lost her shoe,
My master's lost his fiddle-stick
And knows not what to do.

Cock-a-doodle do!
What is my dame to do?
Till master finds his fiddle-stick,
She'll dance without her shoe.

LITTLE MISS MUFFET

Little Miss Muffet
Sat on a tuffet,
Eating her curds and whey.
There came a big spider,
And sat down beside her,
And frightened Miss Muffet away.

BABY DOLLY

Hush, baby, my dolly, I pray you
    don't cry,
And I'll give you some bread and
    some milk by and by,
Or perhaps you like custard or,
    maybe, a tart,
Then to either you're welcome with
    all my heart.

LUCY LOCKET

Lucy Locket lost her pocket,
Kitty Fisher found it,
Nothing in it, nothing in it,
But the binding round it.

LITTLE POLLY FLINDERS

Little Polly Flinders
Sat among the cinders
    Warming her pretty little toes.
Her mother came and caught her,
Whipped her little daughter
    For spoiling her nice new clothes.

ELIZABETH

Elizabeth, Elspeth, Betsy, and Bess,
They all went together to seek a
bird's nest,
They found a bird's nest with five
eggs in,
They all took one, and left four in.

CURLY-LOCKS

Curly-locks, Curly-locks,
    wilt thou be mine?
Thou shalt not wash the dishes,
    nor yet feed the swine,
But sit on a cushion,
    and sew a fine seam,
And feed upon strawberries,
    sugar, and cream.

A CANDLE

Little Nanny Etticoat
In a white petticoat
And a red nose,
The longer she stands,
The shorter she grows.

THE DOVE
AND THE WREN

The dove says coo, coo,
    what shall I do?
I can scarce maintain two.
Pooh, pooh! says the wren,
    I've got ten,
And keep them all like gentlemen.

BOBBY SHAFTOE

Bobby Shaftoe's gone to sea,
With silver buckles on his knee,
He'll come back and marry me,
    Pretty Bobby Shaftoe!
Bobby Shaftoe's fat and fair,
Combing down his yellow hair,
He's my love forever more,
    Pretty Bobby Shaftoe.

MARY'S CANARY

Mary had a pretty bird,
    Feathers bright and yellow,
Slender legs—upon my word
    He was a pretty fellow!

The sweetest note he always sung,
    Which much delighted Mary,
She often, where the cage was hung,
    Sat hearing her canary.

BETTY BLUE

Little Betty Blue
Lost her holiday shoe,
What shall little Betty do?
Give her another
To match the other
And then she'll walk upon two.

THE LITTLE MOPPET

I had a little moppet,
I put it in my pocket,
And fed it with corn and hay.
There came a proud beggar,
And swore he should have her,
And stole my little moppet away.

MY MAID MARY

My maid Mary she minds the dairy,
  While I go a-hoeing and mowing
    each morn,
Gaily runs the reel and the little
    spinning wheel,
  While I am singing and mowing
    my corn.

THE CHILDREN THAT LIVED IN A SHOE

There was an old woman
　　Who lived in a shoe,
She had so many children
　　She didn't know what to do.

But they all were so handsome
And clever, I'm told,
That she wouldn't trade one
For diamonds or gold.

There were middle-size children
And short ones and tall,
And babies with tummies
As round as a ball.

They had blue eyes and brown eyes
And pigtails and curls,
And the boys were all jolly,
And so were the girls.

They each had a dog
    Or a bird or a cat,
A goat or a bunny,
    Or something like that.

They each had a drum
  Or a fiddle-dee-dee,

And a little striped suit
  For a swim in the sea.

They each had a wagon,
A doll or a kite,
So no one was lonely
From morning till night.

They each knew a story,
A song or a rhyme,
A joke or a riddle,
For passing the time.

They each could do handsprings,
And flip-flaps and reels,
And turn a fine somersault,
Head over heels.

They each knew a game
    That was jolly to play,
So they always were merry
    And happy and gay.

The Shoe House they lived in,
Both outside and in,
Was clean as a whistle
And neat as a pin.

From the heel to the toe
It was scoured

and scrubbed,

And painted
 and polished,

And dusted and rubbed.

Willie and Tillie
   And Bennet and Bunn
Washed all the windows
   To let in the sun.

Nancy and Lulubelle
     Dusted the rooms,
And swept the floors clean
     With their own little brooms.

Patrick climbed up
    On the roof, it is said,
And painted the chimney
    A beautiful red.

Sally and Sue
Set the table at three,
And put on the kettle
For making the tea.

Jack ran to the store
Every evening at six,
For lollipops, taffy,
Or peppermint sticks.

Mollie made cookies,
    And jam for their bread,
And baked each a birthday cake
High as his head.

Ann made the puppies
Bonnets and shoes,
And read them a story
Out of the news.

Micky made hats
   For the ponies and goats,
And fed them a sugar lump
   After their oats.

Betty knit sweaters
    And socks for the kittens,
And ironed their hankies,
    And mended their mittens.

"With children so clever,"
The old woman cried,
"I've time for my housework,
And plenty beside!"

So she made them red parasols,
Raincoats and boots,

And caps with a tassel,
And snowballing suits.

She packed them a picnic
    Whenever they asked it,
With ham and bananas
    And pop in a basket.

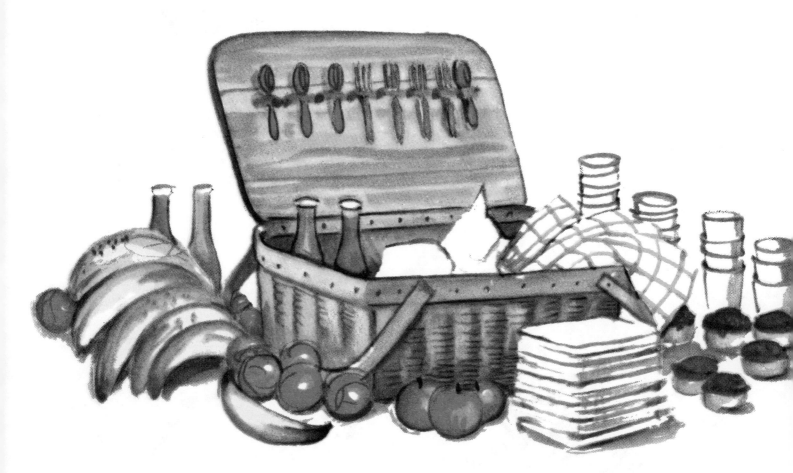

She made them all pocketbooks,
    Just the right size,

With a penny in each
For a special surprise.

"It's jolly as jolly
   To live in a shoe!"
The children all cried
   And the old woman, too!